NATIONAL GEOGRAPHIC

OUR WORLD

THE MIRROR

A Folktale from Korea

Retold by Nick Harris

NATIONAL
GEOGRAPHIC
LEARNING

CENGAGE
Learning·

Tae Hyun, a farmer, is shopping for a present for his wife, Sun Hee.

"I want something very special," he tells a shopkeeper.

"Buy her this mirror," says the shopkeeper. "You can see yourself in it."

At this time in Korea, people did not have mirrors.
"Is that me?" asks Tae Hyun. "I thought I was taller."
Then he says, "No one in my village has one of these.
This is going to be a great present!"

At home, Tae Hyun puts the mirror on the wall.
"Sun Hee is going to love this present!" he says.
"The mirror will show her that she is cuter than
all the other wives in the village."
Tae Hyun goes out to find his wife.

But Sun Hee comes home before Tae Hyun can find her. Tae Hyun's mother is with her.

Sun Hee looks in the mirror. She sees herself for the first time. She thinks it is someone else!

"My husband has a new wife!" she says. "She is younger and prettier than me!"

Tae Hyun's mother looks in the mirror. She sees herself for the first time, too.

"It is not a new wife!" says Tae Hyun's mother. "It is an old woman, like me! But she is even older than me! Your husband has a new mother!"

Tae Hyun's father hears Sun Hee and his wife crying. He comes in to see what is wrong.

"Tae Hyun has a new, younger, and prettier wife!" says Sun Hee.

"No. He has a new, older mother!" says Tae Hyun's mother.

Tae Hyun's father looks in the mirror. He does not recognize himself either.

"It isn't an old woman or a young wife," he says. "It is an old man, like me. But he looks stronger than me!"

"Why does Tae Hyun want a new father?" he asks. "Aren't I strong enough to help him on the farm?"

"I didn't see an old man!" says Sun Hee. "I saw a younger and prettier woman."

"I saw an older woman!" says Tae Hyun's mother.

Tae Hyun and Sun Hee's son comes in. "What is wrong?" he asks.

"Look!" everyone says.

The boy looks in the mirror.

"Who's that boy?" asks the son. "He's wearing my hat! Give me back my hat!"

Finally, Tae Hyun hears his family. He runs into the house. They tell him about the new people they saw in the mirror.

"Those aren't new people!" he says. "You saw yourselves! Look!"

"Ahh!" they all say with a smile. "We are very good looking!"

Facts About Physical Changes: Metamorphosis

The young of some animals do not look at all like the adults they become. They change completely when they become adults. This change is called **metamorphosis.**

Insect Metamorphosis

Some insects change by metamorphosis.

1. A butterfly hatches from an egg. A very tiny caterpillar comes out of the egg.

2. After a while, the caterpillar wraps itself in a covering called a **chrysalis.**

3. After two weeks, a butterfly comes out of the chrysalis.

Amphibian Metamorphosis

Many amphibians also change by metamorphosis.

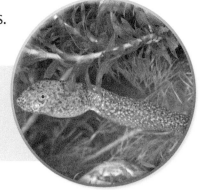

1. A frog baby also hatches from an egg. The baby is called a **tadpole**. It looks like a tiny fish.

2. As time passes, the tadpole grows a head and legs. It starts to look more like a frog.

3. Finally, the frog loses its tadpole tail, and the change is complete. It is no longer a tadpole. It is a frog!

Fun with Families

Write a sentence about the circled person or animal.
Use one of the words below.

> taller   cuter   older
>   stronger   younger

1. _This giraffe_
   is taller.

2. _____
   _____

3. _____
   _____

4. _____
   _____

5. _____
   _____

Write a paragraph about the family in the photo. Use a different word from the box in each sentence.

taller   cuter   older

stronger   younger

The brother is older than the sisters.

_____

_____

_____

_____

Write a few sentences about your own family using the words in the box above.

Glossary

amphibian

amphibians animals that live part of their lives in water and part of their lives on land

hatches comes out of an egg

husband a married man

hatches

insect a type of small animal with a body that has three parts and three pairs of legs

recognize to see someone or something and know who that person or what that thing is

shopkeeper a person who is in charge of a shop or a store

wife a married woman